CW01090900

Mother Hubberd's tale of the fox and ape. Selected from the works of Edmund Spenser. With the obsolete words explained.

Edmund Spenser

ECCO
PRINT EDITIONS

Mother Hubberd's tale of the fox and ape. Selected from the works of Edmund Spenser. With the obsolete words explained.

Spenser, Edmund
ESTCID: T041456
Reproduction from British Library
With a half-title.
London : printed for C. Dilly; and John Stockdale, 1784.
[4],60p. ; 8°

Eighteenth Century
Collections Online
Print Editions

Gale ECCO Print Editions

Relive history with *Eighteenth Century Collections Online*, now available in print for the independent historian and collector. This series includes the most significant English-language and foreign-language works printed in Great Britain during the eighteenth century, and is organized in seven different subject areas including literature and language; medicine, science, and technology; and religion and philosophy. The collection also includes thousands of important works from the Americas.

The eighteenth century has been called "The Age of Enlightenment." It was a period of rapid advance in print culture and publishing, in world exploration, and in the rapid growth of science and technology – all of which had a profound impact on the political and cultural landscape. At the end of the century the American Revolution, French Revolution and Industrial Revolution, perhaps three of the most significant events in modern history, set in motion developments that eventually dominated world political, economic, and social life.

In a groundbreaking effort, Gale initiated a revolution of its own: digitization of epic proportions to preserve these invaluable works in the largest online archive of its kind. Contributions from major world libraries constitute over 175,000 original printed works. Scanned images of the actual pages, rather than transcriptions, recreate the works *as they first appeared.*

Now for the first time, these high-quality digital scans of original works are available via print-on-demand, making them readily accessible to libraries, students, independent scholars, and readers of all ages.

For our initial release we have created seven robust collections to form one the world's most comprehensive catalogs of 18th century works.

Initial Gale ECCO Print Editions collections include:

History and Geography
Rich in titles on English life and social history, this collection spans the world as it was known to eighteenth-century historians and explorers. Titles include a wealth of travel accounts and diaries, histories of nations from throughout the world, and maps and charts of a world that was still being discovered. Students of the War of American Independence will find fascinating accounts from the British side of conflict.

Social Science

Delve into what it was like to live during the eighteenth century by reading the first-hand accounts of everyday people, including city dwellers and farmers, businessmen and bankers, artisans and merchants, artists and their patrons, politicians and their constituents. Original texts make the American, French, and Industrial revolutions vividly contemporary.

Medicine, Science and Technology

Medical theory and practice of the 1700s developed rapidly, as is evidenced by the extensive collection, which includes descriptions of diseases, their conditions, and treatments. Books on science and technology, agriculture, military technology, natural philosophy, even cookbooks, are all contained here.

Literature and Language

Western literary study flows out of eighteenth-century works by Alexander Pope, Daniel Defoe, Henry Fielding, Frances Burney, Denis Diderot, Johann Gottfried Herder, Johann Wolfgang von Goethe, and others. Experience the birth of the modern novel, or compare the development of language using dictionaries and grammar discourses.

Religion and Philosophy

The Age of Enlightenment profoundly enriched religious and philosophical understanding and continues to influence present-day thinking. Works collected here include masterpieces by David Hume, Immanuel Kant, and Jean-Jacques Rousseau, as well as religious sermons and moral debates on the issues of the day, such as the slave trade. The Age of Reason saw conflict between Protestantism and Catholicism transformed into one between faith and logic -- a debate that continues in the twenty-first century.

Law and Reference

This collection reveals the history of English common law and Empire law in a vastly changing world of British expansion. Dominating the legal field is the *Commentaries of the Law of England* by Sir William Blackstone, which first appeared in 1765. Reference works such as almanacs and catalogues continue to educate us by revealing the day-to-day workings of society.

Fine Arts

The eighteenth-century fascination with Greek and Roman antiquity followed the systematic excavation of the ruins at Pompeii and Herculaneum in southern Italy; and after 1750 a neoclassical style dominated all artistic fields. The titles here trace developments in mostly English-language works on painting, sculpture, architecture, music, theater, and other disciplines. Instructional works on musical instruments, catalogs of art objects, comic operas, and more are also included.

The BiblioLife Network

This project was made possible in part by the BiblioLife Network (BLN), a project aimed at addressing some of the huge challenges facing book preservationists around the world. The BLN includes libraries, library networks, archives, subject matter experts, online communities and library service providers. We believe every book ever published should be available as a high-quality print reproduction; printed on-demand anywhere in the world. This insures the ongoing accessibility of the content and helps generate sustainable revenue for the libraries and organizations that work to preserve these important materials.

The following book is in the "public domain" and represents an authentic reproduction of the text as printed by the original publisher. While we have attempted to accurately maintain the integrity of the original work, there are sometimes problems with the original work or the micro-film from which the books were digitized. This can result in minor errors in reproduction. Possible imperfections include missing and blurred pages, poor pictures, markings and other reproduction issues beyond our control. Because this work is culturally important, we have made it available as part of our commitment to protecting, preserving, and promoting the world's literature.

GUIDE TO FOLD-OUTS MAPS and OVERSIZED IMAGES

The book you are reading was digitized from microfilm captured over the past thirty to forty years. Years after the creation of the original microfilm, the book was converted to digital files and made available in an online database.

In an online database, page images do not need to conform to the size restrictions found in a printed book. When converting these images back into a printed bound book, the page sizes are standardized in ways that maintain the detail of the original. For large images, such as fold-out maps, the original page image is split into two or more pages

Guidelines used to determine how to split the page image follows:

• Some images are split vertically; large images require vertical and horizontal splits.
• For horizontal splits, the content is split left to right.
• For vertical splits, the content is split from top to bottom.
• For both vertical and horizontal splits, the image is processed from top left to bottom right.

MOTHER HUBBERD's TALE

OF THE

FOX AND APE·

[PRICE ONE SHILLING.]

MOTHER HUBBERD's TALE

OF THE

FOX AND APE.

SELECTED FROM THE WORKS OF

EDMUND SPENSER,

WITH THE

OBSOLETE WORDS EXPLAINED.

LONDON:

PRINTED FOR C. DILLY, POULTRY; AND JOHN STOCKDALE, PICCADILLY,

MDCCLXXXIV.

MOTHER HUBBERD'S TALE

O F

THE FOX AND APE.

IT was the month in which the righteous Maid,
That for difdain of finful worlds upbraid,
Fled back to Heaven, whence fhe was firft conceived,
Into her filver bower, the fun received,
And the hot *Syrian* dog on him awaiting,
After the chafed lion's cruel baiting,
Corrupted had th' air with his noifom breath,
And pour'd on th' earth plague, peftilence, and death.
Emongft the reft, a wicked malady
Reign'd emongft men, that many did to die,
Depriv'd of fenfe and ordinary reafon ,
That it to *leeches* * feemed ftrange and *geafon.* †

B   My

---

* *Leeches,* phyficians.—† *Geafon,* wonderful.

My fortune was, 'mongſt many others moe,
To be partaker of their common woe;
And my weak body, ſet on fire with grief,
Was robb'd of reſt, and natural relief.
In this ill plight, there came to viſit me
Some friends, who ſorry my ſad caſe to ſee,
Began to comfort me in chearful wiſe,
And means of gladſom ſolace to deviſe.
But ſeeing kindly ſleep refuſe to do
His office, and my feeble eyes forego,
They ſought my troubled ſenſe how to deceave
With talk, that might unquiet fancies reave,
And ſitting all on ſeats about me round,
With pleaſant Tales (fit for that idle *ſtound* *)
They caſt in courſe to waſte the weary hours
Some told of Ladies and their Paramours,
Some of brave Knights and their renowned Squires;
Some of the *Fairies* and their ſtrange attires,
And ſome of Giants, hard to be believed,
That the delight thereof me much relieved.
Amongſt the reſt, a good old Woman was,
Hight † Mother *Hubberd*, who did far ſurpaſs
The reſt in honeſt mirth, that ſeem'd her well
She, when her turn was come her Tale to tell,
Told of a ſtrange adventure, that betided
Betwixt the Fox and th' Ape by him miſguided,

The

* *Stound*, ſituation.—† *Hgb*, called

The which for that my fenfe it greatly pleafed,
All were my fpirit heavy and difeafed,
I'le write in terms, as fhe the fame did fay,
So well as I her words remember may.
No Mufe's aid me needs here-to to call;
Bafe is the ftyle, and matter mean withal.

Whylom * (faid fhe) before the World was civil,
The Fox and th' Ape difliking of their evil
And hard eftate, determined to feek
Their fortunes far abroad, *lyeke with his lyeke* · †
For both were crafty and unhappy witted,
'Two fellows might no where be better fitted.

The Fox, that firft this caufe of grief did find,
'Gan ‡ firft thus plain his cafe with words unkind:
Neighbour Ape, and my Goffip *eke* § befide
(Both two fure bands in friendfhip to be ty'd)
To whom may I more truftily complain
The evil plight that doth me fore conftrain,
And hope thereof to find due remedy?
Hear then my pain and inward agony.
Thus many years I now have fpent and worn,
In mean regard and bafeft fortune's fcorn,

B 2   Doing

---

* *Whylom*, formerly.—† *Lyeke with his lyeke*, for like; fimi-
lar, the one agreeing with the otner.—‡ *'Gan*, began.—
§ *Eke*, alfo, likewife

Doing my country fervice as I might,
No lefs, I dare fay, than the proudeft *wight*, *
And ftill I hoped to be up advanced
For my good parts, but ftill it hath mifchanced,
Now therefore that no longer hope I fee,
But froward fortune ftill to follow me,
And *lofels* † lifted high, where I did look,
I mean to turn the next leaf of the book
Yet ere that any way I do betake,
I mean my Goffip privy firft to make.

Ah! my dear Goffip (anfwer'd then the Ape)
Deeply do your fad words my wits *awhape*, ‡
Both for becaufe your grief doth great appear,
And eke becaufe myfelf am touched near
For I likewife have wafted much good time,
Still waiting to preferment up to clime,
Whilft others always have before me ftept,
And from my beard the fat away have fwept,
That now unto defpair I 'gin § to grow,
And mean for better wind about to throw
Therefore to me, my trufty friend, *aread* ‖
Thy counfel   Two is better than one head.

Certes * (faid he) I mean me to difguize
In fome ftrange habit, after uncouth *wize*, †

Or

---

* *Wight* perfon, a man.—† *Lofels*, fcoundrels.—‡ *Awhape*,
ftrike forcibly, affect — § '*Gin*, begin — ‖ *Aread*, direct —
Certes, certainly.—† *Wize*, fafhion

Or like a pilgrim or a *lymiter*, *
Or like a gipfen, or a juggler,
And fo to wander to the worldes end,
To feek my fortune, where I may it mend.
For worfe than that I have, I cannot meet.
Wide is the world I *wote*, † and every ftreet
Is full of fortunes and adventures ftraunge,
Continually fubject unto chaunge.
Say, my fair Brother now, if this device
Do like you, or may you to like entice.

Surely (faid th' Ape) it likes me wondrous well;
And would ye not poor fellowfhip expell,
Myfelf would offer you t' accompany
In this adventure's chanceful jeopardy,
For to wex old at home in idlenefs
Is difadventrous, and quite fortunelefs.
Abroad where change is, good may gotten be.

The Fox was glad, and quickly did agree
So both refolv'd the morrow next enfuing,
So foon as day appear'd to people's viewing,
On their intended journey to proceed
And over night, what-fo thereto did need,
Each did prepare in readinefs to be
The morrow next, fo foon as one might fee

Light

Light out of Heaven's windows forth to look,
Both their habiliments unto them took,
And put themfelves (a God's name) on their way.
When-as the Ape beginning well to *wey* *
This hard adventure; thus began t' advife.

Now read, Sir *Reynold*, as ye be right wife,
What courfe ye ween is beft for us to take,
That for ourfelves we may a living make
Whether fhall we profefs fome trade or fkill?
Or fhall we vary our device at will,
Even as new occafion appears?
Or fhall we tie ourfelves for certain years
To any fervice, or to any place?
For it behoves, ere that into the race
We enter, to refolve firft hereupon.

Now furely Brother (faid the Fox anon)
Ye have this matter motioned in feafon
For every thing that is begun with reafon
Will come by ready means unto his end;
But things mifcounfelled muft needs *mifwend*. †
Thus therefore I advife upon the cafe,
That not to any certain trade or place,
Nor any man we fhould ourfelves apply;
For, why fhould he that is at liberty

Make

---

* *Wey*, to confider — † *Mifwend*, end badly.

Make himself bond ? *Sith* * then we are free born,
Let us all fervile bafe fubjection fcorn,
And as we be fons of the world fo wide,
Let us our fathers heritage divide,
And challenge to ourfelves our portions dew
Of all the patrimony, which a few
Now hold in hugger-mugger in their hand,
And all the reft do rob of good and land.
For now a few have all, and all have nought,
Yet all be brethren *ylike* † dearly bought
There is no right in this partition,
Ne was it fo by inftitution
Ordained firft, ne by the law of Nature,
But that fhe gave like blefling to each creature,
As well of wordly *livelode* ‡ as of life,
That there might be no difference nor ftrife,
Nor ought call'd mine or thine Thrice happy then,
Was the condition of mortal men
That was the Golden Age of *Saturn* old,
But this might better be the World of Gold,
For, without gold, now nothing will be got
Therefore (if pleafe you) this fhall be our plot
We will not be of any occupation,
Let fuch vile vaffals bo n to bafe vocation
Drudge in the world, and for their living *droyle*, §
Which have no wit to live withouten toyle

But

---

* *Sith*, fince — † *Ylike*, alike — ‡ *Livelod*, livelihood, fub-
fiftence.— § *Droy'*, drudge

But we will walk about the world at pleafure,
Like two free-men, and make our eafe our treafure.
Free-men fome beggars call; but they be free,
And they which call them fo more beggars be ·
For they do *fwink* * and fweat to feed the other,
Who live like Lords of that which they do gather,
And yet do never thank them for the fame,
But as their due by Nature do it clame.
Such will we fafhion both our felves to be,
Lords of the World, and fo will wander free
Where-fo us *lifeth*, † uncontroll'd of any .
Hard is our hap, if we (emongft fo many)
Light not on fome that may our ftate amend ,
Sildom but fome good cometh ere the end.

Well feem'd the Ape to like this ordinaunce ·
Yet well confidering of the circumftaunce,
As paufing in great doubt a while he ftaid,
And afterward with grave advizement faid ;
I cannot, my *lef* ‡ Brother, like but well
The purpofe of the *complot* § which ye tell :
For well *wot* ‖ I (compar'd to all the reft
Of each degree) that beggars life is beft ,
And they that think themfelves the beft of all,
Oft-times to begging are content to fall

But

---

* *Swink*, labour —† *Lifeth*, choofeth.— ‡ *Lief*, beloved
—§ *Complot*, plan, joint plot — ‖ *Wot*, know.

But this I wote withal, that we fhall *ronne* *
Into great daunger, like to be undonne
Wildly to wander thus in the world's eye,
Withouten Pafport or good Warrantye,
For fear left we like rogues fhould be reputed,
And for *ear-mark'd beafts* † abroad be bruted:
Therefore I read, that we our counfels call,
How to prevent this mifchief ere it fall,
And how we may with moft fecurity,
Beg amongft thofe that beggars do defy.

　　Right well, dear Goffip, ye advifed have,
(Said then the Fox) but I this doubt will fave;
For ere we farther pafs, I will devife
A Pafport for us both in fitteft wife,
And by the names of Soldiers us protect;
That row is thought a civil begging fect,
Be you the fouldier, for you likeft are
For manly femblance, and fmall fkill in war:
I will but wait on you, and as occafion
Falls out, myfelf fit for the fame will fafhion.

　　The Pafport ended, both they forward went,
The Ape clad fouldier-like, fit for th' intent,

C

In

In a blue jacket with a crofs of red,
And many flits, as if that he had fhed
Much blood through many wounds therein received,
Which had the ufe of his right arm bereaved ,
Upon his head an old *Scotch* cap he wore,
With a plume feather all to pieces tore
His breeches were made after the new cut ;
Al Portugefe, loofe like an empty gut ,
And his hofe broken high above the heeling,
And his fhooes beaten out with traveling.
But neither fword nor dagger he did bear,
Seems that no foe's revengement he did fear ;
In ftead of them a handfom bat he held,
On which he leaned, as one for in eld. *
Shame light on him, that through fo falfe illufion,
Doth turn the name of fo ildiers to *abufion* , †
And that, which is the nobleft myfterie,
Brings to reproach and common infamie.

Long they thus travelled, yet never met
Adventure which might them a working fet ,
Yet many ays they fought, and many try'd,
Yet for their purpofes none fit efpy'd.
At laft, they chaunc'd to meet upon the way
A fimple Hufband-man in garments gray ,

                                    Yet

* *E d,* in years — † *Abufion,* abufe , fcandal

Yet though his vefture were but mean and bafe,
A good yeoman he was of honeft place,
And for more thrift did care than for gay clothing,
Gay without good, is good hearts greateft loathing.
The Fox him fpying, bad the Ape him *dight* *
To play his part, for loe he was in fight,
That (if he err'd not) fhould them entertain,
And yield them timely profit for their pain.
Eftfoons† the Ape himfelf 'gan to uprear,
And on his fhoulders high his bat to bear,
As if good feryice he were fit to do,
But little *thrift* ‡ for him he did it to:
And ftoutly forward he his fteps did ftrain,
That like a handfom fwain it him became.
When-as they nigh approached, that good man
Seeing them wander loofely, firft began
'T' enquire of cuftom, what and whence they were?
To whom the Ape, I am a Souldiere,
That late in war have fpent my deareft blood,
And in long feryice loft both limbs and good,
And now conftrain'd that trade to over-give,
I driven am to feek fome means to live
Which might it you in pity pleafe t' afford,
I would be ready both in deed and word,

C 2

To

To do you faithful service all my days.
This yron world (that same he weeping says)
Brings down the stoutest hearts to lowest state:
For misery doth bravest minds abeat,
And make them seek for that they wont to scorn,
Of fortune and of hope at once forlorn.

The honest man that heard him thus complain,
Was griev'd, as he had felt part of his pain,
And well dispos'd him some relief to show,
*Askt** if in husbandry he ought did know,
To plough, to plant, to reap, to rake, to sow,
To hedg, to ditch, to thresh, to thatch, to mow,
Or to what labour else he was prepar'd ?
For husband's life is labourous and hard
When-as the Ape him heard so much to talk
Of labour, that did from his liking balk,
He would have slipt the coller handsomly,
And to him said , Good Sir, full glad am I
To take what pains may any living wight
But my late maimed limbs lack wonted might
To do their kindly services as needeth
Scarce this right hand the mouth with diet feedeth,
So that it may no painful work endure
Ne† to strong labour can it self enure,

But

But if that any other place you have,
Which aſks ſmall pains, but thriftineſs to ſave,
Or care to overlook, or truſt to gather,
Ye may me truſt as your own ghoſtly Father.

With that, the Huſband-man 'gan him *avize*, *
That it for him was fitteſt exerciſe
Cattle to keep, and grounds to over-ſee ;
And aſked him if he could willing be
To keep his ſheep, or to attend his ſwine,
Or watch his mares, or take his charge of kine ?

Gladly (ſaid he) whatever ſuch like pain
Ye put on me, I will the ſame ſuſtain
But gladlieſt I of your fleecy ſheep
(Might it you pleaſe) would take on me to keep.
For ere that unto arms I me betook,
Unto my Father's ſheep I us'd to look.
That yet the ſkill thereof I have not loſt ·
There-to right well this curdog by my coſt,
(Meaning the Fox) will ſerve my ſheep to gather,
And drive to follow after their belwether.

The Huſband-man was *meanly* † well content,
Tryal to make of his endeavourment,

And

And home him leading, lent to him the charge
Of all his flock, with liberty full large,
Giving account of the annual increase
Both of their lambs and of their woolly fleece.

Thus is this Ape become a Shepherd Swain,
And the false Fox his dog, (God give them pain)
For, ere the year have half his course out-run,
And do return from whence he first begun,
They shall him make an ill account of thrift,

Now, when-as time flying with winges swift,
Expired had the term, that these two *javels* *
Should render up a reckning of their travels
Unto their master, which it of them sought,
Exceedingly they troubled were in thought ;
Ne wist † what answer unto him to frame,
Ne how to scape great punishment, or shame,
For their false treason and vile thievery.
For, not a Lamb of all their flocks supply
Had they to shew , but ever as they bred,
They slew them, and upon their fleshes fed .
For that disguised dog lov'd blood to spill,
And drew the wicked Shepherd to his will.

So

* *Javels,* worthless fellows.— † *Wist,* knew.

So twixt them both they not a lambkin left,
And when lambs fail'd, the old sheeps lives they *reft*, *
That how t'acquit themselves unto their Lord,
They were in doubt, and flatly *set abord* †
The Fox then counsel'd th' Ape, for to require
Respite till morrow, t' answer his desire ·
For time's delay new hope of help still breeds
The good man granted, doubting not their deeds,
And bade, next day that all should ready be.
But they more subtil meaning had than he
For the next morrow's meed they closely ment,
For fear of afterclaps for to prevent.
And that same evening, when all shrouded were
In carelefs sleep, they without care or fear,
Cruelly fell upon their flock in fold,
And of them slew at pleafure what they *wold* ‡
Of which, when as they feafted had their fill,
For a full complement of all their ill,
They ftole away, and took their hafty flight,
Carry'd in clouds of all concealing night.
So was the Hufband-man left to his lofs,
And they unto their fortune's change to tofs.
After which fort they wandered long while,
Abufing many through their cloaked guile;

That

That at the laft they 'gan to be defcry'd
Of every one, and all their *fleights* * efpy'd,
So as their begging now them failed quite,
For none would give, but all men would them vite:
Yet would they take no pains to get their living,
But feek fome other way to gain by giving
Much like to begging, but much better named,
For many beg, which are thereof afhamed.
And now the Fox had gotten him a gown,
And th' Ape a caffock fide-long hanging down;
For they their occupation meant to change,
And now in other ftate abroad to range
For, fince their Souldier's pafs no better fped,
They forg'd another, as for Clerks book-red
Who paffing forth, as their adventures fell,
Through many *haps*, † which needs not here to tell;
At length chanc'd with a formal Prieft to meet,
Whom they in civil manner fii ft did greet,
And after, afkt an alms for God's dear love
The man ftraight-way his choler up did move,
And with reproachful terms 'gan them revile,
For following that trade fo bafe and vile,
And afkt what licence, or what pafs they had?
Ah (faid the Ape, as fighing wondrous fad)

It's

* *Sleights*, devices, tricks —† *Haps*, chances, accidents

It's an hard cafe, when men of good deferving
Muft either driven be perforce to fterving,
Or afked for their pafs by every *fquib,* *
That lift at will them to revile or *fnib* †
And yet (God wote) fmall odds I often fee
'Twixt them that afk, and them that afked be.
Nath'lefs, ‡ becaufe you fhall not us mifdeem,
But that we are as honeft as we feem,
Ye fhall our pafport at your pleafure fee,
And then ye will (I hope) well moved be.
Which when the Prieft beheld, he view'd it nere,
As if therein fome text he ftudying were,
But little elfe (God wote) could thereof fkill.
For, read he could not evidence, nor will,
Ne tell a written word, ne write a letter,
Ne make one tittle worfe, ne make one better:
Of fuch deep learning little had he need,
Ne yet of *Latin,* ne of *Greek,* that breed
Doubts mongft Divines, and difference of texts,
From whence arife diverfity of fects,
And hateful herefies of God abhor'd
But this good Sir did follow the plain Word,
Ne meddled with their controverfies vain,
All his care was, his fervice well to *fain,* §

D

And

<hr>

* *Squib,* paltry fellow.— † *Snib,* reprimand —‡ *Nath'lefs,*
nevertheless —§ *Sain,* to repeat

And to read Homelies on holidays,
When that was done, he might attend his plays,
An eafy life, and fit High God to pleafe.
He, having overlookt their pafs at eafe,
'Gan at the length them to rebuke again,
That no good trade of life did entertain,
But loft their time in wandring loofe abroad,
Seeing the world, in which they *bootlefs boad,**
Had ways enow for all therein to live,
Such grace did God unto his creatures give.

Said then the Fox; Who hath the world not tride,
From the right way full *cath* † may wander wide
We are but novices new come abroad,
We have not yet the tract of any troad,
Nor on us taken any ftate of life,
But ready are of any to make *prief* ‡
Thererore, might pleafe you, which the world have
     proved,
Us to advife, which forth but lately moved,
Of fome good courfe, that we might undertake·
Ye fhall for ever us your bondmen make.

The Prieft 'gan wex half proud to be fo praid, .
And thereby willing to afford them aid,

                                     It

* *Bootlefs boad,* lived unprofitably — † *Eath,* eafily —
‡ *Prief,* proof

It feems (faid he) right well that ye be *Clerks*, *
Both by your witty words, and by your werks.
Is not that name enough to make a living
To him that hath a whit of Nature's giving?
How many honeft men fee ye arife
Daily thereby, and grow to goodly prize?
To Deans, to Archdeacons, to Commiffaries,
To Lords, to Principals, to Prebendaries,
All jolly Prelates, worthy rule to bear,
Who ever them envie Yet fpite bites near.
Why fhould ye doubt then, but that ye likewife
Might unto fome of thofe in time arife?
In the mean time to live in good eftate,
Loving that love, and hating thofe that hate;
Being fome honeft Curate, or fome Vicar,
Content with little in condition ficker.

Ah! but (faid the Ape) the charge is wondrous
    great,
To feed mens fouls, and hath an heavy threat.
To feed mens fouls (quoth he) is not in man,
For, they muft feed themfelves, do what we can,
We are but charg'd to lay the meat before.
Eat they that lift, we need to do no more,

But

* *Clerks*, Clergymen, Priefts.

But God it is that feeds them with his grace,
The bread of Life pour'd down from heavenly place.
Therefore said he that with the budding rod
Did rule the Jews, *All shall be taught of God.*
That same hath Jesus Christ now to him taught,
By whom the flock is rightly fed and taught.
He is the Shepherd, and the Priest is he,
We but his shepherd swains ordain'd to be
Therefore here-with do not yourself dismay,
Ne is the pains so great, but bear ye may,
For not so great as it was wont of *yore,* *
It's now adays, ne half so straight and sore.
They whylom used duly every day
Their service and their holy things to say,
At morn and even, besides their anthems sweet,
Their peny masses, and their complynes meet,
Their dirges, their *trentals,*† and their shrifts,
Their memoirs, their singings, and their gifts.
Now all these needless works are laid away,
Now once a week upon the Sabbath-day,
It is enough to do our small devotion,
And then to follow any merry motion,
Ne are we tyed to fast, but when we list,
Ne to wear garments base of wollen twist,

But

* *Yore,* formerly —† *Trental,* thirty masses

But with the fineft filks us to aray,
That before God we may appear more gay,
Refembling *Aaron's* glory in his place.
For far unfit it is, that perfons bafe
Should with vile clothes approach God's Majeftie,
Whom no uncleannefs may approachen nie
Or that all men which any Mafter ferve,
Good garments for their fervice fhould deferve,
But he that ferves the Lord of Hoafts moft high,
And that in higheft place, t' approach him nigh,
And all the peoples prayers to prefent
Before his Throne, as on ambaffage fent
Both to and fro, fhould not deferve to wear
A garment better than of wool or hair,
Befide, we may have lying by our fides
Our lovely laffes, or bright fhining brides·
We be not tyde to wilful chaftity,
But have the gofpel of free Liberty.

By that he ended had his ghoftly Sermon,
The Fox was well endued to be a Parfon,
And of the Prieft eftfoons 'gan to enquire,
How to a benefice he might afpire,
Marry there (faid the Prieft) is art indeed;
Much good deep learning one thereout may reed.

For,

For, that the ground-work is, and end of all,
How to obtain a beneficial.
First, therefore, when ye have in handsome wise
Your selves attired, as you can devise,
Then to some noble man your self apply,
Or other great one in the worldes eye,
That hath a zealous disposition
To God, and so to his Religion,
There must thou fashion eke a godly zeale,
Such as no *caspers** may contrayr reveale.
For, each thing fained ought more wary be,
There thou must walk in sober gravitie,
And seem as saint-like as Saint *Radegund*,
Fast much, pray oft, look lowly on the ground,
And unto every one do courtesie meek
These looks (nought saying) do a benefice seek,
And be thou sure one not to lack ere long.
But if thee list unto the Court to throng,
And there to hunt after the hoped prey,
Then must thou thee dispose another way
For there thou needs must learn to laugh, to lye,
To face, to forge, to scoff, to company,
To crouch, to please, to be a beetle-stock
Of thy great Master's will, to scorn, or mock

So

* *Caspers*, cavillers.

So maift thou chance mock out a benefice,
Unlefs thou canft one conjure by device,
Or caft a figure for a Bifhoprick
And if one could, it were but a fchool trick.
Thefe be the ways, by which without reward,
Livings in Courts be gotten, though full hard.
For nothing there is done without a fee
The Courtier needs muft recompenced be
With a benevolence, or have in *gage* *
The *primitias* † of your Parfonage
Scarce can a Bifhoprick forpafs them by,
But that it muft be gelt in privity
Do not thou therefore feek a living there,
But of more private perfons feek elfewhere;
Whereas thou mayeft compound a better peny,
Ne let thy learning queftion'd be of any
For fome good Gentleman that hath the right
Unto his Church for to prefent a wight,
Will cope with thee in reafonable wife·
That if the living yearly do arife
To forty pound, that then his youngeft fon
Shall twenty have, and twenty thou haft won:
Thou haft it won, for it is of frank gift,
And he will care for all the reft to fhift,

Both,

---

† *Gige*, pledge —† *Primitias*, firft fruits

Both, that the Bifhop may admit of thee,
And that therein thou mayeft maintained be.
This is the way for one that is unlearn'd
Living to get, and not to be difcern'd.
But they that are great Clerks, have nearer ways,
For Learning-fake to living them to raife
Yet many eke of them (*God wote**) are driven,
T' accept a benefice in pieces *riven*. †
How fay'ft thou (Friend) have I not well difcourft
Upon this common-place (tho' plain, not wourft) ?
Better a fhort Tale, than a bad long *fhriving*, ‡
Needs any more to learn to get a living ?

Now fure, and by my *Hallidom* § (quoth he)
Ye a great Mafter are in your degree
Great thanks I yield you for your difcipline,
And do not doubt but duly to incline
My wits thereto, as ye fhall fhortly hear
The Prieft him wifh'd good fpeed, and well to fare :
So parted they, as either's way them led
But th' Ape and Fox e'er long fo well them fped,
Through the Prieft's wholefom counfil lately taught,
And through their own fair handling wifely wrought,

That

---

† *God wote*, God know. — ‡ *River*, torn — § *Shriving*,
confeffion —‖ *Hall dom*, holy dame, or lady By my Hallidom, is an oath by my Holy Dame, that is, the Virgin
Mary

That they a benefice 'twixt them obtained,
And crafty *Reynold* was a Prieſt ordained,
And th' Ape his Pariſh-Clark procur'd to be ·
Then made they revel-rout, and goodly glee.
But e'er long time had paſſed, they ſo ill
Did order their affairs, that the evil-will
Of all their Pariſh'ners they had conſtrain'd,
Who to the Ordinary of them complain'd,
How foully they their offices abus'd,
And them of crimes and hereſies accus'd,
That Purſivants he often for them ſent
But they neglecting his commandement,
So long perſiſted obſtinate and bold,
Till at the length he publiſhed to hold
A Viſitation, and them cited thether ·
Then was high time their wits about to gether;
What did they then, but made a compoſition
With their next neighbor Prieſt, for light condition,
To whom their Living they reſigned quight
For a few pence, and ran away by night.
So paſſing through the country in diſguize,
They fled far oft, where none might them ſurprize;
And after that long ſtrayed here and there,
Through every field and foreſt far and near;
Yet never found occaſion for their tourn,
But almoſt *ſterv'd,* * did much lament and mourn.

E

At

* *Sterved,* ſtarved.

At laft, they chanc'd to meet upon the way
The Mule, all deck'd in goodly rich array,
With bells and boffes, that full loudly rung,
And coftly trappings, that to ground down hung.
Lowly they him faluted in meek wife,
But he, through pride and fatnefs, 'gan defpife
Their meannefs ; fcarce vouchfaf'd them to requite.
Whereat the Fox, deep groaning in his fprite,
Said, Ah ! Sir Mule, now bleffed be the day,
That I fee you fo goodly and fo gay
In your attires, and eke your filken hyde
Fill'd with round flefh, that every bone doth hide,
Seems that in fruitful paftures ye do live,
Or fortune doth you fecret favour give.

Foolifh Fox (faid the Mule) thy wretched need
Praifeth the thing that doth thy forrow breed
For well I ween, * thou canft not but envy
My wealth, compar'd to thine own mifery,
That art fo lean and meagre waxen late,
That fcarce thy legs uphold thy feeble gate.

Ay me (faid then the Fox) whom evil hap
Unworthy in fuch wretchednefs doth wrap,

And

* *Ween*, think.

And makes the fcorn of other beafts to be
But lend (fair Sir, of grace) from whence come ye?
Or what of tydings you abroad do hear?
News may perhaps fome good unweeting bear.

From Royal Court I lately came (faid he)
Where all the bravery that eye may fee,
And all the happinefs that heart defire,
Is to be found, he nothing can admire,
That hath not feen that Heaven's pourtraéture.
But tydings there is none, I you affure,
Save that which common is, and known to all,
That Courtiers, as the tide, do rife and fall.

But tell us (faid the Ape) we do you pray,
Who now in Court doth bear the greateft fway:
That if fuch fortune do to us befall,
We may feek favour of the beft of all.

*Marry** (faid he) the higheft now in grace,
Be the wild beafts, that fwifteft are in chace,
For in their fpeedy courfe and nimble flight
The Lion now doth take the moft delight,
But chiefly joys, on foot them to behold,
Enchafte with chain and circulet of gold.

S

* *Marry,* truly.

So wild a beaft, fo tame ytaught to be,
And buxom to his bands is joy to fee.
So well his golden circlet him befeemeth ·
But his late chain his Liege unmeet efteemeth;
For fo brave beafts he loveth beft to fee
In the wild foreft, raunging frefh and free.
Therefore if fortune thee in court to live,
In cafe thou ever there wilt hope to thrive,
To fome of thefe thou muft thy felf apply ·
Elfe, as a thiftle-down in th' air doth fly,
So vainly fhalt thou to and fro be toft,
And lofe thy labour and thy fruitlefs coft.
And yet full few that follow them I fee,
For Vertue's bare regard advaunced be,
But either for fome gainful benefit,
Or that they may for their own turns be fit.
Nath'lefs, perhaps, ye things may handle fo,
That ye may better thrive than thoufands moe.

But (faid the Ape) how fhall we firft come in,
That after we may favour feek to win?

Ho elfe (faid he) but with a good bold face,
And with big words, and with a ftately pace,
That men may think of you in general,
That to be in you, which is not at all.

For

For not by that which is, the world now deemeth
(As it was wont) but by that fame that feemeth.
Ne do I doubt, but that ye well can fafhion
Your felves thereto, according to occafion
So fare ye well, good Courtiers may ye be ;
So proudly neighing, from them parted he.

Then 'gan this crafty Couple to devize,
How for the Court themfelves they might *aguize* *
For thither they themfelves meant to addrefs,
In hope to find there happier fuccefs
So well they fhifted, that the Ape anon
Himfelf had cloathed like a Gentleman,
And the fly Fox, as like to be his groome,
That to the Court in fpeedy fort they come.
Where the fond Ape, himfelf uprearing high
Upon his tiptoes, ftalketh ftately by,
As if he were fome great *Magnifico*,
An boldly doth amongft the boldeft go.
And his Man *Reynold,* with fine *Counterfefaunce,* †
Supports his credit and his countenaunce.
Then 'gan the Courtiers gaze on every fide,
And ftare on him, with big looks *bafen wide,* ‡
Wondring what *mifter wight* § he was, and whence
For he was clad in ftrange accouftrements,

Fafhion'd

* *Aguize,* put on an appearance —† *Counterfefaun* , coun-
terfeiting —‡ *Bafen wide,* looks of wonder —§ *Mifter wight,*
means kind of perfon

Fashion'd with *queint* * devises, never seen
In Court before, yet there are all fashions been:
Yet he them in New-fanglenes did pass.
But his behaviour altogether was
Alla Turchesca, † much the more admir'd,
And his looks loftie, as if he aspir'd
To dignity, and 'sdeign'd the low degree,
That all which did such strangenes in him see,
By secret means 'gan of his state enquire,
And privily his servant thereto hire
Who, throughly arm'd against such coverture,
Reported unto all, that he was sure
A noble Gentleman of high regard,
Which thro' tne world had with long travel far'd,
And seen the manners of all beasts on ground,
Now here arriv'd, to see if like he found.

Thus did the Ape at first him credit gain,
Which afterwards he wisely did maintain
With gallant show, and daily more augment
Through his fine feats and courtly complement,
For he could play, and dance, and vaute, and
        spring,
And all that else pertains to revelling,

Only

* *Queint*, odd, strange —† *Alla Turchesca*, in the Turkish manner

Only through kindly aptneſs of his joints.
Beſides, he could do many other points,
The which in Court him ſerved to good ſtead
For he 'mongſt Ladies could their fortunes read
Out of their hands, and merry leaſings tell,
And juggle finely, that became him well.
But he ſo light was at leger demain,
That what he touch'd came not to light again;
Yet would he laugh it out, and proudly look,
And tell them, that they greatly him miſtook.
So would he ſcoff them out with mockery,
For he therein had great felicity,
And with ſharp _quips_ * joy'd others to deface,
Thinking that their diſgracing did him grace:
So whilſt that other like vain wits he pleaſed,
And made to laugh, his heart was greatly eaſed.
But the right gentle mind would bite his lip,
To hear the javel ſo good men to nip
For though the vulgar yield an open ear,
And common Courtiers love to _gybe_ † and flear
At every thing which they hear ſpoken ill,
And the beſt ſpeeches with ill-meaning ſpill;
Yet the brave Courtier, in whoſe beauteous thought
Regard of honour harbours more than ought,

Doth

* _Quips_, jeſts, ſarcaſms.—† _Gybe_, reproach

Doth loath fuch bafe condition, to backbite
Any's good name for envy or defpite ·
He ftands on terms of honourable mind,
Ne will be carried with the common wind
Of Court's inconftant mutability,
Ne after every tatling fable fly ;
But hears and fees the follies of the reft,
And thereof gathers for himfelf the beft
He will not creep, nor crouch with fained face,
But walks upright with comely ftedfaft pace,
And unto all doth yield due courtefie ;
But not with kiffed hand below the knee,
As that fame apifh crue is wont to do
For he difdains himfelf t' embafe there-to ;
He hates foul *leafings*, * and vile flattery,
Two filthy blots in noble gentery ;
And loathful idlenefs he doth deteft,
The canker-worm of every gentle breft :
The which to banifh, with fair exercife
Of knightly feats, he daily doth devife .
Now menaging the mouths of ftubborn fteeds,
Now practifing the proof of warlike deeds ;
Now his bright arms affaying, now his fpear,
Now the nigh-aimed ring away to bear,

At

* *Leafings*, lies.

At other times he cafts to fue the chace
Of fwift wild beafts, or run on foot a race,
T' enlarge his breath (large breath in arms moft
　　　　needful)
Or elfe by wreftling to wex ftrong and heedful;
Or his ftiff arms to ftretch with eughen bow,
And many legs ftill paffing to and fro,
Without a gowned beaft him faft befide.
A vain enfample of the Perfian pride,
Who after he had won th' Affyrian foe,
Did ever after fcorn on foot to go.
Thus when this courtly gentleman, with toil
Himfelf hath wearied, he doth recoil
Unto his reft, and there with fweet delight
Of mufick's fkill revives his toiled fpright,
Or elfe with Loves, and Ladies gentle fports,
The joy of youth, himfelf he recomforts.
Or laftly, when the body lift to paufe,
His mind unto the Mufes he withdraws;
Sweet Lady Mufes, Ladies of Delight,
Delights of life, and ornaments of light,
With whom he clofe confers with wife difcourfe,
Of Nature's works, of Heaven's continual courfe,
Of foreign lands, of people different,
Of kingdom's change, of divers government,
Of dreadful battails, of renowned Knights,
With which he kindleth his ambitious fprights

To like defire and praife of noble fame,
The only up-fhot whereto he doth aim
For all his mind on Honour fixed is,
To which he levels all his purpofes,
And in his Prince's fervice fpends his days,
Not fo much for to gain, or for to raife
Himfelf to high degree; as for his grace,
And in his hking to win worthy place,
Through due deferts, and comely carriage,
In whatfo pleafe employ his perfonage,
That may be matter meet to gain him praife;
For he is fit to ufe in all aflays,
Whether for arms and warlike amenance,
Or elfe for wife and civil governance;
For he is practiz'd well in policy,
And thereto doth his courting moft apply ·
To learn the *enterdeale* * of Princes ftrange,
To mark th' intent of counfels, and the change
Of ftates, and eke of private men fome-while,
Supplanted by fine falfhood and fair guile,
Of all the which he gathereth what is fit
T'enrich the ftorehoufe of his powerful Wit,
Which through wife fpeeches, and grave conference
He daily ekes, and brings to excellence.

Such

* *Enterdeale,* mediation

Such is the rightful Courtier in his kind,
But unto such the Ape lent not his mind,
Such were for him no fit companions,
Such would defcry his leud conditions
But the young lufty gallants he did chofe
To follow, meet to whom he might difclofe
His witlefs pleafance, and ill-pleafing vein.
A thoufand ways he them could entertain,
With all the thriftlefs games that may be found,
With *mumming* ⸱ and with mafking all around,
With dice, with cards, with balliards far unfit,
With fhuttlecocks, miffeeming manly wit,
With courtizans, and coftly *riotize*, †
Whereof ftill fomewhat to his fhare did rize
Ne them to pleafure, would he fometimes fcorn
A pandar's coat (fo bafely was he born,)
There-to he could fine loving verfes frame,
And play the Poet oft.   But ah! for fhame,
Let not fweet Poets praife, whofe only pride
Is vertue to advance, and *vive* ‡ deride,
Be with the work of *lofils* § wit defamed,
Ne let fuch verfes poetry be named
Yet he the name on him would rafhly take,
Maugre ‖ the facred Mufes, and it make

F 2

A fer-

---

* *Mumming*, originally Spanifh, it means frolicking in
difguife —† *Riotize*, debauchery —‡ *Vive*, lively, forcible.
—§ *Lofils*, a fcoundrel, a forry, worthlefs fellow —‖ *Maugre*,
in fpite of, notwithftanding

A fervant to the vile affection
Of fuch, as he depended moft upon;
And with the fugry fweet thereof allure
Chafte Ladies ears to fantafies impure
To fuch delights the noble Wits he led
Which him reliev'd, and their vain humours fed
With fruitlefs follies, and unfound delights.
But if perhaps into their noble fprights,
Defire of honour, or brave thought of arms
Did ever creep, then with his wicked charms
And ftrong conceits, he would it drive away,
Ne fuffer it to houfe there half a day.
And when-fo love of letters did infpire
Their gentle wits, and kindle wife defire,
That chiefly doth each noble mind adorn,
Then he would fcoff at Learning, and eke fcorn
The *Sectaries* * thereof, as people bafe,
And fimple men, which never came in place
Of world's affairs, but in dark corners *mew'd*, †
Mutter'd of matters, as their books them fhew'd,
Ne other knowledge ever did attain,
But with their gowns their gravity maintain.
From them he would his impudent lewd fpeach
Againft God's Holy Minifters oft reach,

And

---

* *Sectaries*, followers.—† *Mew'd*, confined

And mock Divines and their profeſſion ·
What elſe then did he by progreſſion,
But mock high God himſelf, whom they profeſs ?
But what car'd he for God or godlineſs ?
All his care was himſelf how to advance,
And to uphold his courtly countenance
By all the cunning means he could deviſe ;
Were it by honeſt ways, or otherwiſe,
He made ſmall choice yet ſure his honeſty
Got him ſmall gains, but ſhameleſs flattery,
And filthy *brocage*,* and unſeemly ſhifts,
And borrow baſe, and ſome good Ladies gifts
But the beſt help, which chiefly him ſuſtain'd,
Was his Man *Reyno'd*'s purchaſe which he gain'd.
For he was ſchool'd by kind in all the ſkill
Of cloſe conveyance, and each practice ill
Of *cooſinage* and cleanly knavery,
Which oft maintain'd his Maſter's bravery.
Beſides, he us'd another ſlippery ſleight,
In taking on himſelf in common fight
Falſe perſonages, fit for every ſted,
With which he thouſands cleanly cooſined
Now like a merchant, merchants to deceave,
With whom his credit he did often leave

In

---

* *Brocage*, gain gotten by bargains —† *Cooſinage*, cozenage.

In *gage*,* for his gay Master's hopeless *det* †
No like the lawyer, when the land would let,
Or sell fee-simples in his master's name,
Which he had never, nor ought like the same ·
Then would he be a broker, and draw in
Both wares and money, by exchange to win
Then would he seem a farmer, that would sell
Bargains of woods, which he did lately fell,
Or corn, or cattle, or such other ware,
There-by to coosin men not well aware,
Of all the which there came a secret fee
To th' Ape, that he his countenance might be.
Besides all this, he us'd oft to beguile
Poor suters, that in Court did haunt some while,
For he would learn their business secretly,
And then inform his Master hastily,
That he by means might cast them to prevent,
And beg the sute the which the other ment,
Or otherwise, false *Reynold* would abuse
The simple suter, and wish him to chuse
His Master, being one of great regard
In Court, to compass any sute not hard,
In case his pains were recompenc'd with reason:
So would he work the silly man by treason

To

---

* *Gage*, pledge —† *Det*, debt.

To buy his Master's frivolous good-will.
That had not power to do him good or ill.

So pitiful a thing is futers state!
Moft miferable man, whom wicked fate
Hath brought to Court, to fue for *had-ywift,**
That few have found, and many one hath mist,
Full little knoweft thou that haft not tride,
What hell it is, in fuing long to bide,
To lofe good days that might be better fpent,
To wafte long nights in penfive difcontent
To fpeed to-day, to be put back to-morrow,
To feed on hope, to pine with fear and forrow,
To have thy Prince's Grace, yet want her Peers;
To have thy afking, yet wait many years,
To fret thy foul with croffes and with cares,
To eat thy heart through comfortlefs defpairs,
To fawn, to crouch, to wait, to ride, to ronne,
To fpend, to give, to want, to be undonne.
Unhappy wight, born to difaftrous end,
That doth his life in fo long tendence fpend.
Whoever leaves fweet home, where mean eftate
In fafe affurance, without ftrife or hate,
Finds all things needful for contentment meek,
And will to Court, for fhadows vain to feek,

Or

---

* *Had-ywift,* a phrafe peculiar to Spenfer, it means, " I
" wifh I had "

Or hope to gain, himself a daw will try ·
That curse God send unto mine enemy.
For none but such as this bold Ape unblest,
Can ever thrive in that unlucky quest,
Or such as hath a *Reynold* to his Man,
That by his shifts his Master furnish can.

But yet this Fox could not so closely hide
His crafty feats, but that they were descride
At length, by such as sate in Justice Seat,
Who for the same him foully did entreat,
And having worthily him punished,
Out of the Court for ever banished.
And now the Ape wanting his *Huckster-man,* *
That wont provide his necessaries, 'gan
To grow into great lack, ne could up-hold
His countenance in those his garments old ;
Ne new ones could he easily provide,
Though all men him uncased 'gan deride,
Like as a Puppit placed in a Play,
Whose part once past, all men bid take away
So that he driven was to great distress,
And shortly brought to hoplefs wretchednefs.
Then closely as he might, he cast to leave
The Court, not asking any pafs or leave,

But

* *Huckster-man,* his provider

But ran away in his rent rags by night,
Ne ever ftaid in place, ne fpake to wight,
Till that the Fox his *copefmate* * he had found,
To whom complaining his unhappy *ftound*, †
At laft again with him in travel join'd,
And with him far'd fome better chance to find.
So in the world long time they wandered,
And *mickle* ‡ want and hardnefs fuffered ;
That them repented much fo foolifhly
To come fo far to feek for mifery,
And leave the fweetnefs of contented home,
Though eating hips, and drinking watry fome.

Thus as they them complained to and fro,
Whil'ft through the forreft *rechlefs* § they did go,
Lo where they fpide, how in a gloomy glade,
The Lion fleeping lay, in fecret fhade,
His Crown and Sceptre lying him befide,
And having *doft* ‖ for heat his dreadful hide ·
Which when they faw, the Ape was fore afraid,
And would have fled with terror all difmaid .
But him the Fox with hardy words did ftay,
And bad him put all cowardize away ,
For now was time (if ever they would hope)
To aim their counfels to the faireft fcope,

G

And

---

* *Copefmate*, companion and friend —† *Stound*, fituation —
‡ *Mickle*, much, great —§ *Rechlefs*, carelefs —‖ *Doft*, put off.

And them for ever highly to advaunce,
In cafe the good which their own happy chaunce
Them freely offred, they would wifely take.

Scarce could the Ape yet fpeak, fo did he quake,
Yet as he could, he afkt how good might grow,
Where nought but dread and death do feem in fhow?

Now (faid he) whiles the Lion fleepeth found,
May we his Crown and Mace take from the ground,
And eke his fkin, the terror of the wood,
Where-with we may our felves (if we think good)
Make Kings of beafts, and Lords of forrefts all,
Subject unto that Power Imperial.
Ah! but (faid th' Ape) who is fo bold a wretch,
That dare his hardy hand to thofe out-ftretch,
When, as he knows his *meed*, * if he be fpide,
To be a thoufand deaths, and fhame befide?

Fond Ape (faid then the Fox) into whofe breft
Never crept thought of honour nor brave geft,
Who will not venture life a King to be,
And rather rule and raign in foveraign fee,
Than dwell in duft inglorious and bafe,
Where none fhall name the number of his place?

One

---

* *Meed*, reward.

One joyous hour in blisful happinefs,
I chufe before a life of wietchednefs.
Be therefore councelled herein by me,
And fhake off this vile-hearted *cowardree.* *
If he awake, yet is not death the next,
For we may colour it with fome pretext
Of this, or that, that may excufe the crime:
Elfe we may fly, thou to a tree mayft clime,
And I creep undei ground, both from his reach:
Therefore be rul'd to do as I do teach.

The Ape, that *earft* † did nought but chill and
        quake,
Now 'gan fome courage unto him to take,
And was content to attempt that enterprife,
Tickled with glory and rafh *covetife,* ‡
But firft 'gan queftion, whethei fhould affay
Thofe royal ornaments to fteal away.

Marry that fhall your felf (*quoth* § he thereto)
Foi ye be fine and nimble it to do,
Of all the beafts which in the forrefts be,
Is not a fitter for this turn than ye ·
Therefore, mine own dear Brother, take good hart,
And evei think a kingdom is your part.

G 2   Loth

---

* *Cowardree,* cowardice —† *Earft,* a while ago —‡ *Cove-*
tife, avarice, covetous —§ *Quoth,* faid

Loth was the Ape (though praifed) to adventure,
Yet faintly 'gan into his work to enter,
Afraid of every leaf that ftirr'd him by,
And every ftick that underneath did lie,
Upon his tiptoes nicely he up went,
For making noife, and ftill his ear he lent
To every found that under Heaven blew,
Now went, now ftept, now crept, now backward
    drew,
That it good fport had been him to have ey'd ·
Yet at the laft (fo well he him apply'd)
Through his fine handling, and his cleanly play,
He all thofe royal figns had ftoln away,
And with the Fox's help, them borne afide,
Into a fecret corner unefpide,
Whither whenas they came, they fell at words,
Whether or them fhould be the Lord of Lords
For th' Ape was ftrifeful, and ambicious,
And the Fox guileful, and moft covetous,
That neither pleafed was to have the Reign
Twixt them divided into even twain,
But either (algates*) would be Lords alone.
For love and lordfhip bide no *paragone* †

                I am

---

* *A'gates*, on any terms —† *Paragone*, equal

I am moſt worthy (ſaid the Ape) ſith I
For it did put my life in jeopardy,
There-to I am in perſon and in ſtature
Moſt like a Man, the Lord of every Creature.
So that it ſeemeth I was made to raign,
And born to be a Kingly Soveraign

Nay (ſaid the Fox) Sir Ape, you are aſtray.
For tho' to ſteal the Diadem away
Were the work of your nimble hand, yet I
Did firſt deviſe the plot by policy,
So that it wholly ſpringeth from my wit
For which alſo I claim my ſelf more fit
Than you, to rule for Government of State
Will without wiſdom ſoon be ruinate.
And where ye claim your ſelf for outward ſhape
Moſt like a Man, Man is not like an Ape
In his chier parts, that is, in wit and ſpirit,
But I therein moſt like to him do merit,
For my ſly wyles and ſubtile craftineſs,
The title of the kingdom to poſſeſs.
Nath'leſs (my Brother) ſince we paſſed are
Unto this point, we will appeaſe our jar,
And I with reaſon meet will reſt content,
That ye ſhall have both Crown and Government,

Upon

* *Nath leſs*, nevertheleſs

Upon condition that ye ruled be
In all affairs, and councelled by me;
And that ye let none other ever draw
Your mind from me, but keep this as a law:
And hereupon an oath unto me plight.

The Ape was glad to end the strife so light;
And there-to swore   for who would not oft swear,
And oft unswear, a Diadem to bear?
Then freely up those royal spoils he took,
Yet at the Lion's skin he inly *quook*, *
But it dissembled, and upon his head
The crown, and on his back the skin he did,
And the false Fox him helped to array.
Then when he was all *dight*,† he took his way
Into the forrest, that he might be seen
Of the wild beasts in his new glory *sheen*. ‡
There the two first, whom he encountred, were
The Sheep and th' Ass, who striken both with fear
At sight of him, 'gan fast away to fly;
But unto them the Fox aloud did cry,
And in the King's name bade them both to stay,
Upon the pain that thereof follow may.
Hardly nath'less were they restrained so,
Till that the Fox forth toward them did go,

And

* *Quook*, did quake — † *Dight*, dressed, decked.— ‡ *Sheen*
shining with splendour

And there diffuaded them from needlefs feai,
For that the King did favour to them beai,
And therefore dreadlefs bade them come to Court.
For no wild beafts fhould do them any *torte*, *
There or abroad, ne would his Majefty
Ufe them but well, with gracious clemency,
As whom he knew to him both faft and true,
So he perfuaded them with homage due
Themfelves to humble to the Ape proftrate,
Who gently to them bowing in his gate,
Received them with chearful entertain.

Thence, forth proceeding with his princely train,
He fhortly met the Tyger and the Boai,
Which with the fimple Camel raged fore
In bitter words, feeking to take occafion,
Upon his flefhy corps to make invafion
But foon as they this Mock-King did efpy,
Their troublous ftrife they ftinted by and by,
Thinking indeed that it the Lion was.
He then to prove whether his power would pafs
As currant, fent the Fox to them ftraightway,
Commanding them their caufe of ftrife *bewiay* ; †
And if that wrong on either fide there were,
That he fhould warn the wronger to appear

The

The morrow next at court, it to defend,
In the mean time upon the King t'attend.

    The subtile Fox so well his message said,
That the proud beasts him redily obey'd
Whereby the Ape in wondrous stomach wox,   *
Strongly encourag'd by the crafty Fox,
That King indeed himself he shortly thought,
And all the beasts him feared as they ought
And followed him into his palace he,   †
Where taking *congee*, ‡ each one by and by
Departed to his home in dreadful awe,
Full of the feared fight which late they saw.

    The Ape thus seized of the regal throne,
Eftsoons, by councel of the Fox alone,
'Gan to provide for all things in assurance,
That so his rule might longer have endurance.
First, to his gate he pointed a strong guard,
That none might enter but with issue hard.
Then for the safeguard of his personage,
He did appoint a warlike equippage
Of forrain beasts, not in the forrest bred,
But part by land, and part by water fed.

Γor

For tyranny is with ftrange aid fupported.
Then unto him all monftrous beafts reforted
Bred of two kinds, as Griffons, Minotaures,
Crocodiles, Dragons, Beavers, and Centaures :
With thofe himfelf he ftrengthened mightily,
That fear he need no force of enemy.
Then 'gan he rule and tyrannize at will,
Like as the Fox did guide his gracelefs fkill ;
And all wild beafts made vaffals of his pleafures,
And with their fpoils enlarg'd his private treafures.
No care of juftice, nor no rule of reafon,
No temperance, nor no regard of feafon,
Did thenceforth ever enter in his mind ;
But cruelty, the fign of currifh kind,
And 'fdainful pride, and wilful arrogaunce ,
Such follows thofe whom fortune doth advaunce.
But the falfe Fox moft kindly plaid his part
For, whatfoever mother Wit, or Art
Could work, he put in proof. no practice fly,
No counterpoint of cunning policy,
No reach, no breach, that might him profit bring,
But he the fame did to his purpofe wring.
Nought fuffered he the Ape to give or graunt,
But through his hand alone muft pafs the *fiaunt.* *

H   All

* *Fiaunt,* warrant.

All offices, all leafes by him lept,
And of them all what-fo he lik'd, he kept.
Juftice he fold, injuftice for to buy,
And tor to purchafe for his progeny.
Ill might it profper, that ill gotten was,
But fo he got it, little did he pafs.
He fed his cubs with fat of all the foil,
And with the fweet of others fweating toil,
He crammed them with crums of benefices,
And fill'd their mouths with meeds of *malefices*, *
He cloathed them with all colours, fave white,
And loaded them with Lordfhips and with might,
So much as they were able well to bear,
That with the weight their backs nigh broken were,
He chaffred chairs in which churchmen were fet,
And breach of laws to privy farm did let.
No ftatute fo eftablifhed might be,
Nor ordinance fo needful, but that he
Would violate, though not with violence,
Yet under colour of the confidence
The which the Ape repos'd in him alone,
And reckned him the kingdom's corner ftone.
And ever, when he ought would bring to pafs,
His long experience the platform was.

And

* *Malfices*, evil deeds

And when he ought not pleafing would put by,
The cloke was care of thrift, and hufbandry,
For to encreafe the common treafure's ftore ;
But his own treafure he encreafed more,
And lifted up his lofty towres thereby,
That they began to threat the neighbour fky ,
The whiles the Prince's palaces fell faft
To ruin   (for what thing can evei laft ?)
And whil'ft the othei Peers for poverty
Were forc't their ancient houfes to let lie,
And their old caftles to the ground to fall,
Which their forefathers famous over all,
Had founded for the kingdom's ornament,
And for their memories long *moniment,**
But he no count made of Nobility,
Nor the wild beafts whom arms did glorify,
The realm's chief ftrength and *g rlond*† of the Crown ;
All thefe through famed crimes he thruft adown,
Or made them dwell in darknefs of difgrace
For none, but whom he lift, might come in place.
Of men of arms he had but fmall regard,
But kept them low, and ftreightned very hard,
For men of learning little he efteemed ,
His wifdom he above their learning deemed,

H 2

As

Moniment, monument.—† *Gulond,* garland.

As for the rafcal commons leaft he cared,
For not fo common was his bounty fhared;
Let God (faid he) if pleafe, care for the many,
I for myfelf muft care before elfe any
So did he good to none, to many ill,
So did he all the Kingdom rob and pill,
Yet none durft fpeak, nor none durft of him *plain*, *
So great he was in grace, and rich through gain.
Ne would he any let to have accefs
Unto the Prince, but by his own addrefs
For all that elfe did come, were fure to fail,
Yet would he further none but for avail.
For on a time the fheep, to whom of yore
The Fox had promifed of friendfhip ftore,
What time the Ape the Kingdom firft did gain,
Came to the Court, her cafe there to complain,
How that the Wolf, her mortal enemy,
Had fithence flain her lamb moft cruelly,
And therefore crav'd to come unto the King,
To let him know the order of the thing.
Soft, gooddy fheep (then faid the Fox) not fo.
Unto the King fo rafh you may not go,
He is with greater matter bufied
Than a lamb, or the lamb's own mother's hed

Ne

* *Plain*, complain

Ne certes may I take it well in part,
That ye my coufin Wolf fo foully thwart,
And feek with flander his good name to blot·
I or there was caufe, elfe do it he would not.
Therefore *furceafe*, * good Dame, and hence depart·
So went the fheep away with heavy heart.
So many *moe*,† fo every one was ufed,
That to give largely to the box refufed.

Now when high *Jove*, in whofe almighty hand,
The care of Kings and Powers of Empires ftand,
Sitting one day within his turret hie,
From whence he views with his black-lidded eye,
What-fo the Heaven in his wide vault contains,
And all that in the deepeft earth remains,
And troubled kingdom of wild beaits beheld,
Whom not their kindly fovereign did weld, ‡
But an ufurping Ape with guile fuborn'd,
Had all fubvert, he fdeignfully it fcorn'd
In his great heart, and hardly did refrain,
But that with thunderbolts he had him flain,
And driven down to Hell, his dueft meed
But him avifing, he that dreadful deed
Forebore, and rather chofe, with fcornful fhame,
Him to avenge, and blot his brutifh name

Unto

---

* *Surceafe*, leave off, refrain —† *Moe*, more, a great number —‡ *Weld*, govern

Unto the world, that never after any
Should of his race be void of infamy
And his falfe Counfellor, the caufe of all,
To damn to death, or *dole** perpetual,
From whence he never fhould be quit, nor ftall'd.
Forth-with he *Mercury* unto him call'd,
And bade him fly with never-refting fpeed
Unto the forreft, where wild beafts do breed,
And there enquiring privily, to learn
What did of late chance to the Lion *ftearn*,†
That he ru.l'd not the Empire, as he ought;
And whence were all thofe plaints unto him brought,
Of wrongs and fpoils by falvage beafts committed;
Which done, he bade the Lion be remitted
Into his feat, and thofe fame treachours vile
Be punifhed for their prefumptuous guile.
The fon of *Maia*, foon as he receiv'd
That word, ftraight with his azure wings he cleav'd
The liquid clouds and lucid firmament,
Ne ftaid, till that he came with fteep defcent
Unto the place, where his prefcript did fhow.
There ftouping like an arrow from a bow,
He foft arrived on the graffie plain,
And fairly paced forth with eafie pain,

Till

Till that unto the palace nigh he came,
Then 'gan he to himfelf new fhape to frame,
And that fair face, and that ambrofial hue,
Which wonts to deck the gods immortal crew,
And beautifie the fhiny firmament,
He doft, unfit for that rude *rabblement* *
So ftanding by the gates in ftrange difguize,
He 'gan enquire of fome in fecret wize,
Both of the King and of his government,
And of the Fox, and his falfe blandifhment,
And evermore he heard each one complain
Of foul abufes both in realm and raign
Which yet to prove more true, he meant to fee,
And an eye-witnefs of each thing to be.
Tho' on his head his dreadful hat he dight,
Which maketh him invifible to fight,
And mocketh th' eyes of all the lookers on,
Making them think it but a vifion
Through power of that, he runs through enemies
   fwerds,
Through power of that, he paffeth through the herds
Of ravenous wild beafts, and doth beguile
Their greedy mouths of the expected fpoil;
Through power of that, his cunning thieveries
He wonts to work, that none the fame efpies,
        And

* *Rabblement*, croud.

And through the power of that, he putteth on
What shape he lift in apparition.
That on his head he wore, and in his hand
He took *Caduceus* his snaky wand,
With which the damned ghosts he governeth,
And furies rules, and *Tartare* tempereth.
With that he causeth sleep to seize the eyes,
And fear the hearts of all his enemies;
And when him lift, an univerfal night
Throughout the world he makes on every wight,
As when his sire with *Alcumena* lay.
Thus dight, into the court he took his way,
Both through the gard, which never him descride,
And through the watchmen, who him never spide;
Thence, forth he past into each secret part,
Whereas he saw (that sorely griev'd his hart)
Each place abounding with foul injuries,
And fill'd with treasure rack'd with robberies.
Each place defil'd with blood of guiltless beasts,
Which had been slain to serve the Ape's *beheasts*. *
Gluttony, malice, pride, and covetize,
And lawlesness raigning with riotize,
Besides the infinite extortions
Done through the Fox's great oppressions,

That

* *B beasts*, commands

That the complaints thereof co'd not be told
Which when he did with loathful eyes behold,
He would no more endure, but came his way,
And ca'lt to feek the Lion where he may,
That he might work th' avengement for his fhame,
On thofe two *caitives** which had bred him blame.
And feeking all the foreft bufil,
At laft he found, where fleeping he did lie,
The wicked weed, which there the Fox did lay,
From underneath his head he took away,
And then him waking, forced up to rife,
The Lion looking up, 'gan him *avize* †
As one late in a trance, what had or long
Become of him, for fantafie is ftrong
Arife (faid *Mercury*) thou fluggifh beaft,
That heareft fenflefs, like the corpfe deceaft,
The whilft thy kingdom from thy head is rent,
And thy Throne Royal with difhonour blent
Arife, and do thyfelf redeem from fhame,
And be aveng'd on thofe that breed thy blame,
There at enraged foon he 'gan up-ftart,
Grinding his teeth, and grating his great hart,
And rouzing up himfelf for his revenge
He 'gan to reach, but no where it efpie

I

There-

Caitives, mean flaves, defpicable knaves —† *Aviz*, behold, obferve

There-with he 'gan full terribly to roar,
And *chaf'd* at that indignity right fore
But when his Crown and Scepter both he wanted,
Lord how he fum'd, and swell'd, and rag'd, and
     panted,
And threatned death, and thousand deadly dolours
To them that had purloin'd his princely honours'
With that in haste, disrobed as he was,
He towards his own palace forth did pass,
And all the way he roared as he went,
That all the forrest with astonishment
Thereof did tremble, and the beasts therein
Fled fast away from that so dreadful din.
At last, he came unto his mansion,
Where all the gates he found fast lockt anon,
And many warders round about them stood
With that he roar'd aloud, as he were *wood,*†
That all the palace quaked at the stound,
As if it quite were riven from the ground,
And all therein were dead and heartless left,
And th' Ape himself, as one whose wits were *reft,*‡
Fled here and there, and every corner sought,
To hide himself from his own feared thought.
But the false Fox, when he the Lion heard,
Fled closely forth, straightway of death afear'd,

           And

---

* *Chaf't,* became enraged —† *Wood,* mad.—‡ *Reft,* lost

And to the Lion came full lowly creeping,
With fained face, and watry *eyn**** half weeping,
To excufe his former treafon and abufion,
And turning all unto the Ape s confufion :
Nath'lefs, the royal beaft forbore believing,
But bade hi n ftay at cafe till further *prieving.*†
Then when he faw no entrance to him graunted,
Roaring yet loudei that all hearts it daunted,
Upon thofe gates with force he fiercely flew,
And rending them in pieces, felly flew
Thofe warders ftrange, and all that elfe he met.
But th' Ape ftill flying, he no where might get ;
From room to room, from beam to beam he fled
All breathlefs, and for fear now almoft ded
Yet him at laft the Lion fpide, and caught,
And foi th with fhame unto his judgment brought.
Then all the beafts he caus'd affembled be,
To hear their doom, and fad enfample fee .
The Fox, firft author of that treachery,
He did uncafe, and then away let fly :
But th' Ape's long tail (which then he had) he quite
Cut off, and both ears pared of their height ,
Since which, all Apes but half their ears have left,
And of their tails are utterly bereft.

So

So Mother *Hubberd* her difcourfe did end
Which pardon me, if I amifs have pen'd,
For, weak was my remembrance it to hold,
And bad her tongue that it fo bluntly told.

I I N I S

www.ingramcontent.com/pod-product-compliance
Ingram Content Group UK Ltd.
Pitfield, Milton Keynes, MK11 3LW, UK
UKHW051609190125
4177UKWH00042B/725